CW00585430

it's a treat to have a friend like you

by max & lucy®

Time Warner Books

WARNER BOOKS

An AOL Time Warner Company

Time Warner Books are published by
AOL Time Warner Book Group
1271 Avenue of the Americas
New York, N.Y. 10020

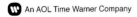 An AOL Time Warner Company

10 9 8 7 6 5 4 3 2 1
ISBN:1-931722-12-9
Printed in the United Kingdom

Who else but a friend

They know our little secrets. They see through our antics and attitudes. They're our friends, and without them, well, life wouldn't be quite as rich.

This little book is about those few folks who somehow get into our lives and change them for the better. We certainly know we don't always make it easy on them. But somehow, they hang in there with us anyway. It's amazing.

If you're reading this, someone has either given this book to you or you're about to give it to someone else. Either way, you and your friend both get a reason to celebrate. And we're honored to be a little part of it. Cheers!

max & lucy®

a few thoughts
of your own

it's a treat to have
a friend like you...

...because...

your friendship is the ultimate gift

psst. without you, life would stink

sometimes i'm a crab.
thanks for not cracking

thanks for being a loyal friend

you appreciate my bad side

you keep me moving!

i'm glad you're in my future

even when i'm trashed,
you don't throw me away

thanks for your support

you're an angel

without you,
my bowl is empty

to me, you'll always be royalty

thanks for all you do

you make me soar

having you as a friend
is the smartest move i've made

thanks for making me
always feel at home

this much

love our funky friendship

a friend like you
is the best reward

hats off to a great friend

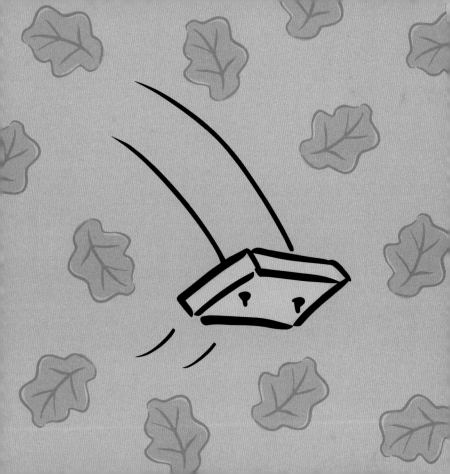

thanks for enduring
my mood swings

you add style
to our friendship

i can be a flake,
thanks for being patient

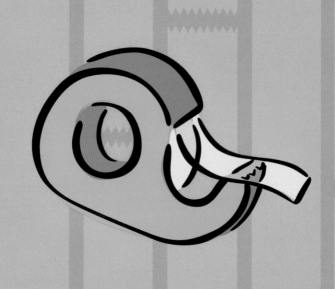

friends like us
always stick together

heartfelt thanks
to a cherished friend

you're a bright spot in my life

We're a pair

thanks for seeing
the butterfly inside me

i'm nuts about you

i can be a pest.
thanks for not swatting

you're great to hang with

thanks for dealing
with my hang-ups

without you, i'd be sunk

you make me feel like a star

it's a treat to have
a friend like you

acknowledgments

The entire staff at Max & Lucy helped make this book possible, and we thank them all. We offer special acknowledgment to Bradley Smith and Aaron Thompson for their witty designs and perpetual can-do attitudes. To our families and friends who continue to believe in us, we share our gratitude. And, of course, to our friends at AOL Time Warner Books, who made this entire project possible, we send our deepest appreciation.

max & lucy

about max & lucy

Max & Lucy is a tiny little company in Phoenix, Arizona, that makes greeting cards, notes and other fun ways for people to correspond. Founded by Russ Haan and named after two cats who live in a warehouse, the company is now owned by Russ and two good friends, Mike Oleskow and Bradley Smith. As the author in the crowd, Russ penned most of this book, but humbly admits that without his partners, the words would not have been the same. To learn more about Max & Lucy, feel free to visit the company's web site at www.maxandlucy.com.

max & lucy®